C000130367

International Finance Discussion Papers: The Sovereignty Option: The Quebec Referendum and Market Views on the Canadian Dollar

United States Federal Reserve Board,
Michael P. Leahy, Charles P. Thomas

The BiblioGov Project is an effort to expand awareness of the public documents and records of the U.S. Government via print publications. In broadening the public understanding of government and its work, an enlightened democracy can grow and prosper. Ranging from historic Congressional Bills to the most recent Budget of the United States Government, the BiblioGov Project spans a wealth of government information. These works are now made available through an environmentally friendly, print-on-demand basis, using only what is necessary to meet the required demands of an interested public. We invite you to learn of the records of the U.S. Government, heightening the knowledge and debate that can lead from such publications.

Included are the following Collections:

Budget of The United States Government
Presidential Documents
United States Code
Education Reports from ERIC
GAO Reports
History of Bills
House Rules and Manual
Public and Private Laws

Code of Federal Regulations
Congressional Documents
Economic Indicators
Federal Register
Government Manuals
House Journal
Privacy act Issuances
Statutes at Large

Board of Governors of the Federal Reserve System

International Finance Discussion Papers

Number 555

June 1996

THE SOVEREIGNTY OPTION:
THE QUEBEC REFERENDUM AND MARKET VIEWS ON THE CANADIAN DOLLAR

Michael P. Leahy and Charles P. Thomas

NOTE: International Finance Discussion Papers are preliminary materials circulated to stimulate discussion and critical comment. References in publications to International Finance Discussion Papers (other than an acknowledgment that the writer has had access to unpublished material) should be cleared with the author or authors.

ABSTRACT

We use exchange traded options on Canadian dollar futures to estimate the market's risk-neutral distribution for the Canadian dollar in the days before and after the Quebec sovereignty referendum. We employ a relatively new technique that places little a-priori structure on the estimated distribution. This lack of structure allows the estimated distribution to reflect the multi-modal nature of expectations associated with the referendum's results. The technique is especially suited to circumstances in which a particular event will reduce a large degree of uncertainty prior to the expiration date of the options. Our estimated distributions are consistent with a significant perceived probability that the Canadian dollar would move up or down by as much as 5 percent as a result of the vote.

THE SOVEREIGNTY OPTION:
THE QUEBEC REFERENDUM AND MARKET VIEWS ON THE CANADIAN DOLLAR

Michael P. Leahy and Charles P. Thomas[*]

I. Introduction

Sentiment concerning the outcome of the October 1995 sovereignty referendum in Quebec seemed to have a significant impact on the Canadian dollar and Canadian interest rates in the period running up to the referendum. We use options prices on Canadian dollar futures to examine market sentiment about the effect of the referendum on the Canadian dollar.

Options prices are useful because they can provide a fuller description of the expected future distribution of asset prices than is available from forward or futures prices, which represent only the central tendency of a distribution of outcomes. In particular, in situations where the outcome of a single prospective event, such as the referendum, may have discrete and distinct effects on future asset prices, options data can provide information about the range of expected outcomes and the probabilities associated with those outcomes. This feature of options data was exploited by Bates (1990) to assess the probability of a stock market crash and Malz (1995) to estimate realignment probabilities in the EMS.

---

[*] Correspondence should be directed to C. Thomas, Mail Stop #42, Federal Reserve Board, Washington DC 20551; Tel: (202) 452-3698; Fax: (202) 452-6424; Email: thomasc@frb.gov. The authors are staff economists in the Division of International Finance, Board of Governors of the Federal Reserve System. This paper represents the views of the authors and should not be interpreted as reflecting the views of the Board of Governors of the Federal Reserve System or other members of its staff. We thank Carol Bertaut and participants in the IF Monday workshop for their helpful comments. Kevin Huennekens provided valuable research assistance.

Extracting this type of information from options prices requires a method that is sufficiently flexible to accommodate distributions with varying degrees of kurtosis and skewness, and even multiple modes. We use a method developed and applied by Melick and Thomas (1992 and 1996) that incorporates the information in a broad range of available options prices and permits the estimation of a flexibly parameterized distribution function. The advantage of this technique is that it imposes little structure on the process by which exchange rates evolve and permits the estimation of relatively flexible forms for the distribution. In addition, because no specific assumptions need be made about the process for the exchange rate, the method is applicable without modification to situations characterized by jump processes or other discrete changes in exchange rate behavior through time.

As with any method that extracts information about beliefs from financial data, our results require careful interpretation. An option's price, like any asset's price, is influenced by market participants' preferences toward risk as well as beliefs. As such, the distributions recovered from option prices are influenced by risk premia, just as spot and forward rates are. The distributions reported below are the risk-neutral, or martingale-equivalent, distributions consistent with observed asset prices. They differ from the true distributions that market participants had in mind because they incorporate attitudes towards risk in addition to beliefs.

We find that as the referendum drew near and the prospects for its success shifted, there were dramatic changes in the shape of the implied distribution for the future value of the Canadian dollar. Immediately preceding the referendum, the distribution was multi-modal and the implied impact of the vote on the Canadian dollar was consistent with particularly large future movements in the exchange rate. We also find that more standard techniques for recovering the implicit distribution of future values are ill-suited for describing market views in situations like that in the period prior to the Quebec referendum.

The rest of the paper is organized as follows: section II provides background on movements in Canadian interest rates and exchange rates during the period prior to and immediately after the referendum; section III describes the technique of Melick and Thomas (MT) for estimating risk-neutral distributions from options prices; section IV describes the estimation of risk-neutral distributions for Canadian dollar futures and presents the results; and section V summarizes the paper.

II. Events Around the Time of the Referendum

In the second and third quarters of 1995, it appeared that the Canadian dollar, shown in the top panel of chart 1, may have been supported at least in part by a lessening of concerns over the possibility of secession by Quebec, and short-term interest rates in Canada declined both absolutely and relative to comparable U.S. rates. Moving into October, however, these trends began to reverse as polls suggested increasing support for the Quebec separatists. The Canadian dollar declined 3 percent against the U.S. dollar in the four weeks immediately preceding the referendum, and yield spreads on Canadian-U.S. ten-year government bonds increased 30 basis points on balance over the same period. The Canadian-U.S. three-month interbank interest rate spread widened more than 80 basis points, as investors positioned themselves for the possibility that the Bank of Canada would move to offset the effect on monetary conditions of any sharp fall in the currency that might occur following a yes vote on the referendum.[1]

In the month of the referendum, the Canadian dollar was particularly vulnerable to what appeared to be growing support for sovereignty, as indicated in the frequent public opinion polls. In the days immediately preceding the referendum, the province-wide polls showed about 45 percent of Quebec voters openly in support of sovereignty, slightly over 40 percent openly against, and about 15 percent undecided or unwilling to answer the question, with a margin of error of 3 percent or more. Reports of the results of smaller daily polls also circulated in the market. These showed similar percentages narrowly favoring the yes camp, although the margin of error was considerably larger.

More detail on the movements of the Canadian dollar in the days immediately preceding the referendum can be seen in chart 2. The Canadian currency declined sharply on Friday October 20. The decline was sparked by the release late on October 19 of the results of an Angus Reid poll showing the sovereignty supporters ahead by a narrow margin. Canadian interest rates, shown in the lower panel, also began to move substantially higher. A Leger poll out over the subsequent weekend pushed the Canadian dollar lower still on Monday October 23. The Canadian currency hit bottom on the following Tuesday and stayed roughly at that lower level through to Friday October 27. Canadian interest rates also remained elevated throughout the week. The following Monday, the day of the referendum, the Canadian dollar recovered slightly, and Canadian interest rates eased, although the

---

[1] The referendum question was: "Do you agree that Quebec should become sovereign, after having made a formal offer to Canada for a new economic and political partnership, within the scope of the Bill respecting the future of Quebec and the agreement signed on June 12, 1995?"

referendum results were not available until after the close of normal trading in North America. On Tuesday, after it was known that the sovereignty question had been narrowly defeated,[2] the Canadian dollar moved sharply higher, and Canadian interest rates fell. In addition, the Bank of Canada responded to the recovery of the Canadian dollar by reducing its call money target range 25 basis points.

On balance, the Canadian dollar strengthened about 1-1/2 percent between the Friday before the vote and the Tuesday following it. In the days immediately prior to the referendum, some market commentators had suggested that the Canadian dollar could rise or fall 5 percent or more, depending on the outcome of the vote. Was that a realistic assessment (that just failed to come to bear because the vote was so close) or an exaggerated claim (sought out by journalists looking for a dramatic story)? Exchange rates, interest rates, and other asset prices reflect the central tendencies of a distribution of outcomes but do not provide information on the range or perceived probabilities of these outcomes. In this paper, we look to prices of options over a range of strike prices for answers to these questions. In particular, we use options on Canadian dollar futures to gauge the likely range of perceived outcomes following the October 30 referendum and the perceived probabilities associated with those outcomes.

III. The MT Method

In this section, we discuss several issues associated with using options prices to infer market distributions, and we describe the MT method.

---

[2]The final results showed 49.4 percent for the proposition and 50.6 percent against.

Using options prices to make inferences about the higher moments of an asset's distribution is not new. Early efforts relied on the model of Black and Scholes (1973), which prices an option under the assumption that the price of the underlying asset evolves according to geometric Brownian motion. Using an observed option price, together with a risk-free interest rate and the spot price for the underlying asset, the Black-Scholes equation can be inverted to solve for the unknown parameters of the underlying process. These parameters, in turn, describe the lognormal distribution consistent with geometric Brownian motion. There are several well known problems with using the Black-Scholes model, or its commodity analogue (Black (1976)), to infer an asset's distribution. Two concern us here. First, the Black-Scholes model applies to European-style options rather than the more common American-style. Second, observed prices are often inconsistent with the lognormal assumption. Observed asset returns often display excess kurtosis, or fat tails, relative to the assumed distribution. In addition, prices for options that differ only by their strike prices typically imply different estimates for the volatility of the underlying process. That is, at a point in time, the options prices themselves are not consistent with the lognormal assumption of Black-Scholes.

In principle the link between options prices and the distribution is very direct, and it is not necessary to assume lognormality or place any *a priori* structure on a distribution to extract the information in options prices. As shown by Breeden and Litzenburger (1978), if options were traded along a continuum of strikes ranging from zero to infinity, the risk-neutral distribution of the underlying asset is completely described by the second derivative of the option price with respect to the strike price. In practice, however, the fact that options are traded with discrete strike prices and, more importantly, that the range of strike prices is limited, requires us to place some *a priori* structure on the distribution. The method used here assumes that the underlying distribution can be approximated by a mixture of lognormal distributions.[3]

The direct link between the risk-neutral distribution and options prices is severed when we move from European- to American-style options. American options can be exercised anytime prior to their expiration date, implying that their value is determined by the entire stochastic process for the underlying asset rather than its terminal distribution alone. In principle, two different processes that have the same terminal distribution will yield different prices for American-style options. To deal with this feature of American options, we construct upper and lower bounds on the price of the American option conditional on the terminal distribution alone. These bounds are then used in the estimation of the terminal distribution.

All options-based techniques for extracting implicit distributions, except perhaps the Black-Scholes, rely on the fact that the prices of options with different strikes are derived from views about different parts of a single distribution at a given point in time. To reconstitute the different parts into a single distribution requires simultaneous quotes. Settlement prices for exchange-traded options on futures provide a readily available set of simultaneous quotes for the end of the day. Synchronized prices for options on spot currency

---

[3] Simply taking differences of available options prices (the Longstaff (1990) method) can lead to implausible distributions with negative probabilities. Neuhaus (1995) describes a differencing method which avoids this problem. Rubenstein (1994), Shimko (1991), and Aït-Sahalia and Lo (1995) describe other methods to impose structure on the distribution.

are not so readily available. For this reason the method is tailored to American options on futures.

To describe the estimation technique, we first describe how we would estimate the implicit distribution if European-style options were available, and then describe the modifications made to accommodate American-style options.

Estimation of Risk-Neutral Distribution from European Options

Let $c_t[X]$ be the price of a European call option with t days remaining until expiration and a strike price of X. Similarly, let $p_t[X]$ be the price of a European put option. Let f_t be the price of the underlying futures contract t days before the options expire. If the futures price at expiration. f_0, is greater than the strike price, the call option has a value of $f_0 - X$, and the put option has a value of zero. On the other hand, if the futures price is less than the strike price, the call option has a value of zero, and the put option has a value of $X - f_0$. Thus:

$$c_0[X] = \max[f_0 - X. 0], \text{ and} \tag{1}$$

$$p_0[X] = \max[X - f_0, 0]. \tag{2}$$

Cox and Ross (1976) show that, for days prior to expiration, these options prices can be written as a function of a probability density $\gamma[f_0]$ of the underlying futures price at expiration. This density is the risk-neutral density and will differ from the true unconditional density to the extent that it incorporates risk premia. Let $\gamma_t[f_0]$ be the density on a given day, and let $\bar{\rho}_t$ be the risk-free discount rate for the period from day t to day 0. Then, the options prices are given by:

$$c_t[X] = \bar{\rho}_t \int_0^\infty \gamma_t[f_0] \max[f_0 - X, 0] \, df_0 \, , \text{ and} \tag{3}$$

$$p_t[X] = \bar{\rho}_t \int_0^\infty \gamma_t[f_0] \max[X - f_0, 0] \, df_0 \, . \tag{4}$$

To estimate $\gamma[\cdot]$, suppose that it can be approximated by a parametric density function $g[\cdot \, ; \theta_t]$, where $\theta_t \in \Theta_t$ is a vector of parameters that may change from day to day. Let $c_t[X; \theta_t]$ be the call price that results from using the approximate density, and let $p_t[X; \theta_t]$ be the resulting put price:

$$c_t[X; \theta_t] = \bar{\rho}_t \int_0^\infty g[f_0; \theta_t] \max[f_0 - X, 0] df_0, \text{ and} \tag{5}$$

$$p_t[X; \theta_t] = \bar{\rho}_t \int_0^\infty g[f_0; \theta_t] \max[X - f_0, 0] df_0. \tag{6}$$

Define the errors in pricing the options as:

$$e_t^c[X; \theta_t] = c_t[X] - c_t[X; \theta_t] \, , \text{ and} \tag{7}$$

$$e_t^p[X; \theta_t] = p_t[X] - p_t[X; \theta_t] \, . \tag{8}$$

Let X_c and X_p denote the sets of call and put strikes available on a given day. We estimate the distribution by finding the vector $\hat{\theta}_t$ that minimizes squared pricing errors:

$$\hat{\theta}_t \equiv \operatorname*{argmin}_{\theta_t} \sum_{X \in X_c} e_t^c[X; \theta_t]^2 + \sum_{X \in X_p} e_t^p[X; \theta_t]^2 . \qquad (9)$$

Modifications for American Options

Because American-style options can be exercised at any time up to and including their expiration date, they include a premium for early exercise. To allow for this premium, we construct bounds on the prices of American options and estimate the American option price as a weighted average of those bounds. This modification allows for the early exercise premium without imposing unwarranted structure on the stochastic process for the underlying futures exchange rate.[4]

As shown in MT, the martingale property of futures prices allows us to bound the price of an American option in terms of the terminal distribution alone as follows:

$$C_t''[X] = \max\left[E_t[f_0] - X, \ \rho_t \cdot E_t\left[\max[0, f_0 - X]\right]\right], \qquad (10)$$

$$C_t'[X] = \max\left[E_t[f_0] - X, \ \overline{\rho}_t \cdot E_t\left[\max[0, f_0 - X]\right]\right], \qquad (11)$$

---

[4] The standard modification for Americanness used in the literature, Barone-Adesi and Whaley (1987), is applicable only to the case of Brownian motion.

$$P_t^u[X] = \max\left[X - E_t[f_0], \; \rho_t \cdot E_t[\max[0, X - f_0]]\right], \text{ and} \qquad (12)$$

$$P_t^l[X] = \max\left[X - E_t[f_0], \; \bar{\rho}_t \cdot E_t[\max[0, X - f_0]]\right], \qquad (13)$$

where the upper case symbols $C_t^i[X]$ and $P_t^i[X]$ ($i = u, l$) refer to call and put prices for American options, where $E_t[\cdot]$ refers to expectations at time t taken with respect to the risk-neutral distribution at the expiry of the option, and where ρ_t is the one-period discount rate at period t.[5]

The American option price will be a weighted average of the upper and lower bounds. A natural way to interpret where within the bounds the actual option price falls is in terms of how quickly the market expects uncertainty about the future value of the underlying asset to be resolved. If the market expects the uncertainty to be resolved relatively quickly, early exercise is more likely and the option's value will be closer to the upper bound. On the other hand, if traders expect the uncertainty to be resolved later, early exercise is a less valuable feature and the option will be priced nearer to the lower bound. The weights $w_{t,X}^C$ and $w_{t,X}^P$ correspond to the expected speed of this resolution, so that:

---

[5] Note that the bounds differ only by the discount factor used in the second item in the outside max list. Given the relatively short time to expiration of the options used here, the upper and lower bounds are quite close together, with a maximum difference of about 1-1/2 percent. As shown in Chaudhury and Wei (1994) and Melick and Thomas (1996), in continuous time the upper bounds for calls and puts collapse to the undiscounted European value, e.g. $C_t^u[X] = E_t[\max[0, f_0 - X]]$.

$$C_t[X] \equiv w_{t,x}^C \cdot C_t^u[X] + (1 - w_{t,x}^C) \cdot C_t^l[X], \text{ and} \tag{14}$$

$$P_t[X] \equiv w_{t,x}^P \cdot P_t^u[X] + (1 - w_{t,x}^P) \cdot P_t^l[X], \tag{15}$$

where $w_{t,x}^i$, $(i = C, P)$ lie in the unit interval.

For reasons of parsimony, we simplify the above specification and use only two weights, $w_{t,1}$ and $w_{t,2}$, in the estimation. The first is for in-the-money options (those with value if exercised today), and the second is for out-of-the-money options. These weights can be combined with the approximation to the risk-neutral distribution to yield approximate option prices:

$$C_t[X; \theta_t, \boldsymbol{w}_t] \equiv w_{t,i} \cdot C_t^u[X; \theta_t] + (1 - w_{t,i}) \cdot C_t^l[X; \theta_t], \text{ and} \tag{16}$$

$$P_t[X; \theta_t, \boldsymbol{w}_t] \equiv w_{t,i} \cdot P_t^u[X; \theta_t] + (1 - w_{t,i}) \cdot P_t^l[X; \theta_t], \tag{17}$$

where $\boldsymbol{w}_t = (w_{t,1}, w_{t,2})$ and $i = \begin{pmatrix} 1 \text{ if } \begin{pmatrix} call \text{ and } X < E_t[f_0] \\ put \text{ and } X > E_t[f_0] \end{pmatrix} \\ 2 \text{ otherwise} \end{pmatrix}.$

As with the European case, we can construct a pricing error for each option:

$$e_t^{\,c}[X;\theta_t,w_t] = C_t[X] - C_t[X;\theta_t,w_t], \text{ and} \tag{18}$$

$$e_t^{\,p}[X;\theta_t,w_t] = P_t[X] - P_t[X;\theta_t,w_t]. \tag{19}$$

We then estimate (θ_t, w_t) with $(\hat{\theta}_t, \hat{w}_t)$ as follows:

$$(\hat{\theta}_t, \hat{w}_t) = \underset{\theta_t, w_t}{\operatorname{argmin}} \sum_{X \in X_c} e_t^{\,c}[X;\theta_t,w_t]^2 + \sum_{X \in X_p} e_t^{\,p}[X;\theta_t,w_t]^2 \tag{20}$$

Equation (20) describes a non-linear least-squares estimator for the parameters of the risk-neutral distribution and the weights.

IV. Estimation of Futures Distribution

To estimate distributions for Canadian dollar futures, we assume the risk-neutral distribution $\gamma[\cdot]$ can be approximated by a mixture of three lognormal distributions. The assumed distribution . $g[\cdot]$. takes the following form:

$$g[f_0] = \pi_1 g_1[f_0] + \pi_2 g_2[f_0] + \pi_3 g_3[f_0], \tag{21}$$

where

$$g_i[f_0] = \left(\frac{1}{\sqrt{2\pi}\ \sigma_i f_0}\right) \cdot \exp\left[\left(\frac{\ln(f_0) - \mu_i}{\sigma_i}\right)^2 / 2\right], \text{ and} \qquad (22)$$

$$\sum \pi_i = 1, \text{ and } 1 \geq \pi_i \geq 0, \ i = 1, 2, 3.$$

This functional form is appealing because it can reproduce the single lognormal of Black-Scholes as a special case[6] while also readily accommodating leptokurtic, skewed, and multi-modal distributions.

Data

The principal data used in this exercise are the daily settlement prices of December options on the December 1995 Canadian dollar (C$) futures contract traded on the Chicago Mercantile Exchange. The options expired on December 9, 1995, 40 days after the Quebec sovereignty referendum. We estimate distributions from several days in October: October 2, four weeks before the referendum; four days in the 2-week period before the referendum; and October 31, the day after the referendum. Some summary statistics for these data are shown in the table below. The only other data needed for the estimation of the densities are discount factors, which are taken from the prices of the U.S. Treasury bill that matured on December 14, 1995.

---

[6] Strictly speaking, this is Black's 1976 commodity analogue of the Black-Scholes model.

Date	Number of Options		Number of Unique Strikes	Range of Strikes (UScents/C$)
	Calls	Puts		
2 October	16	14	19	69.0 - 78.0
19 October	17	13	19	69.5 - 78.5
20 October	17	16	21	68.5 - 78.5
23 October	17	17	22	68.0 - 78.5
27 October	19	18	23	67.5 - 78.5
31 October	18	13	19	69.0 - 78.0

Estimation Results

Chart 3 shows the estimated densities for three dates. The dramatic change in sentiment about the Canadian dollar from early October to the day before the referendum is reflected in the densities for October 2 and October 27. The probability mass under the density for October 27 is generally to the left of that for the October 2 density, consistent with the depreciation of the Canadian dollar in the runup to the Quebec sovereignty referendum. However, as is apparent from the shapes of the two densities, the shift of the probability mass during the period was not uniform. The density for October 27 shows a much wider dispersion, measured as the distance between the 1/6 and 5/6 quantiles relative to the futures rate. This measure is displayed in the table below the chart. The increase in dispersion over the four-week period occurred despite the tendency of options distributions to become more concentrated as the time to expiration diminishes. The widening in the dispersion reflects the sharp increase in perceived uncertainty about the outcome of the referendum as poll results released during the period showed increasing support for the separatist movement. The level of uncertainty displayed in the density for October 27 is consistent with a 30 percent probability that the Canadian dollar futures rate could rise or fall 5 percent or more following the referendum, more than double the probability of such a move on October 2.

The shape of the density for October 27 seems to indicate three distinct views on the outcome of the referendum. The modal segment of the density, which includes the contemporaneous futures rate, may reflect the market's view that the referendum result would not be a surprise and that the futures rate, which represents the central tendency of the distribution of possible outcomes, would not move much in the remaining days of the option's life. The hump to the right of the mode is consistent with the possibility that the referendum would result in a clear defeat for the sovereignty movement and the Canadian dollar would strengthen significantly. On the other hand, the broad shoulder to the left of the mode may reflect the possibility of a resounding yes for sovereignty, weakening the Canadian dollar significantly. The table below the chart shows implied probabilities that the futures rate will fall below various thresholds.

The density for October 31, the day after the referendum, is shifted back to the right, as the Canadian dollar strengthened following the defeat of the sovereignty referendum. Furthermore, the density is considerably more concentrated, reflecting the elimination of the uncertainty about the outcome of the referendum. In fact, for this date, a mixture of two lognormals fits the data about as well as a mixture of three. Consequently, the density for October 31 shown in chart 3 is estimated with a mixture of only two lognormals.

More detail on the shift in the densities over time is shown in chart 4. The top left panel shows densities for October 2, before the dramatic rise in uncertainty about the outcome of the referendum, and October 20, the day after the release of the Angus Reid poll showing that a plurality of Quebec voters favored sovereignty. Between the two days, probability mass moved from values of the Canadian dollar above $0.75 to values just below that price and into the left tail, consistent with more discreteness in market views about the outcome of the referendum. The top right panel, which shows the density for October 23 along with the October 20 density, shows even more discreteness. Overall, the probability mass shifted further to the left in that Friday-to-Monday period, and distinct humps developed to either side of the mode. These changes followed the release of a Leger poll that showed supporters of sovereignty continued to hold a narrow margin over those opposed. This pattern is consistent with the market view that on October 20 the futures price was generally expected to remain in its then-current neighborhood, with the rest of the probability spread more evenly over a wide range of other outcomes--both higher and lower. The density for October 27, the Friday before the referendum, is shown in the bottom left panel. Apparently, some of the negative sentiment for the Canadian dollar unwound during that week, as probability mass shifted from the left hump to the right. The bottom right panel shows the density for the Tuesday following the Monday referendum. It shifted to the right, consistent with the strengthening of the Canadian dollar following the referendum, and became more concentrated, as the uncertainty associated with the referendum passed.

While changes in risk premia can distort the day-to-day interpretation of these risk-neutral densities in ways that can camouflage changes in market expectations, the shifts in these densities over time nonetheless appear to be consistent with market commentary on the Canadian dollar during the period and may provide some quantitative guidance as to the range of outcomes considered by investors and the perceived likelihood of those outcomes.

In circumstances in which a large amount of uncertainty might be resolved following a specific event like the Quebec referendum, fitting mixtures of lognormals is particularly informative. To compare the results of the approach taken here with the more typical approach, we re-estimated the densities for the several days by fitting a single lognormal distribution to the options data. To isolate the effect of the mixture of lognormals on the estimation results, we used the same methodology to correct for the early exercise premium (i.e., the "bounds" methodology) in both approaches.

The table below compares the sum of the squared pricing errors using the two methods for each of the dates. While it is not surprising that the ratio of the sum of squared pricing errors for the two approaches is always greater than one, it is clear that the ability of the single lognormal to fit the options price data successively deteriorates relative to that of the mixture of lognormals in the days leading up to the October 30 referendum. Immediately following referendum, the ratio drops considerably.[7]

_____

[7]Even though the mixture of three lognormals for October 31 performs somewhat better in terms of squared pricing errors, its improved fit is largely the result of devoting one of the lognormal distributions to explaining options at a single strike price (73.5). In terms of the number of times it produced a smaller prediction error, the mixture of three lognormals performed only marginally better than the mixture of two lognormals. For 17 of the 31 options prices used on October 31, the mixture of three lognormals produced a smaller absolute prediction error than the mixture of two lognormals. We choose to report the results for the mixture of two lognormals in the table because it seems that for this date the extra parameters do not materially improve the overall fit.

| Date | Sum of Squared Pricing Errors (x 10^3) | | Ratio (a/b) |
	Single Lognormal (a)	Lognormal Mixture (b)	
2 October	0.6897	0.3985	1.731
19 October	1.6812	0.4327	3.714
20 October	21.9954	4.5577	4.826
23 October	45.3733	2.9345	16.462
27 October	41.5988	1.3072	31.822
31 October	2.2768	0.8141	2.797

Note. The sum of squared pricing errors under the column marked lognormal mixture is from a mixture of three lognormals for all days except for October 31. For that date, the sum of squared errors is the result of fitting a mixture of two lognormals to the data. With three lognormals, the sum of squared pricing errors for October 31 is 0.3457 x 10^{-3} and the corresponding ratio is 6.586.

Charts 5 through 9 provide additional detail on how the two approaches compare on the various days. The top panel of chart 5 shows the densities that result from using the data for October 2. On that day, which occurred before the substantial increase in uncertainty about the outcome of the referendum, the shapes and the overall ranges of the two densities are roughly similar, although the single lognormal puts a bit more probability mass on higher values of the futures rate than the mixture of lognormals. In addition, the pricing errors of the two approaches, shown in the middle and bottom panels, are fairly similar.

The differences between the two approaches become more dramatic on October 20, shown in chart 6. The densities have markedly different shapes, as the single lognormal is unable to portray the emerging discreteness in the market's views on possible outcomes. The density given by the mixture of lognormals has more probability mass over the two-penny interval containing the futures rate, less probability mass over intervals beginning a penny higher or lower than the futures rate, and about the same probability mass over intervals four pennies away. The inflexibility of the single lognormal shows through to the pricing errors associated with the standard approach. In situations in which investors actually expect some discreteness in outcome and assign probability in a relatively lumpy fashion, the constraint of the smooth bell shape from the single lognormal leads to persistent overpricing or underpricing of options for intervals of strike prices. This pattern of pricing errors is even more evident in charts 7 and 8, where the options data seem to be calling for more discreteness in the distribution of outcomes. As shown in chart 9, however, the differences in the two approaches essentially disappear on the day following the referendum, as the single lognormal and the mixture of lognormals produce roughly equivalent densities and similar pricing errors.

V. Summary and Conclusions

This paper applies a method developed by Melick and Thomas using a mixture of lognormal distributions to study the market's view of the effect on the Canadian dollar of the Quebec sovereignty referendum. It is shown that, in the runup to the vote, uncertainty about the Canadian dollar widened significantly, corroborating market commentary in the days immediately preceding the referendum that the Canadian dollar could rise or fall 5 percent or more as a result of the vote. Furthermore, the shape of the risk-neutral density immediately preceding the day of the referendum exhibits a pattern consistent with three types of outcomes: no surprise, surprising defeat of the sovereignty proposal, and a surprising victory.

It is also shown that, in circumstances in which a particular event will resolve a large degree of uncertainty prior to the expiration of a set of options, the standard practice of fitting a single lognormal density to options prices rather than the more flexible mixture of lognormals can obscure interesting features of the data and force large and persistent pricing errors over ranges of strike prices.

References

Aït-Sahalia, Y., and A. W. Lo. "Nonparametric Estimation of State-Price Densities Implicit in Financial Asset Prices." *NBER Working Paper Series*, 5351 (1995).

Barone-Adesi, G., and R. Whaley. "Efficient Analytic Approximation of American Option Values." *Journal of Finance*, 42 (1987), 301-320.

Bates, D. S. "The Crash of '87: Was It Expected? The Evidence From Options Markets." *Journal of Finance*, 46 (July 1990), 1009-1044.

Black, F. "The Pricing of Commodity Contracts." *Journal of Financial Economics*, 3 (1976), 167-179.

Black, F., and M. Scholes. "The Pricing of Options and Corporate Liabilities." *Journal of Political Economy*, 81 (1973), 637-659.

Breeden, D., and R. Litzenberger. "Prices of State-Contingent Claims Implicit in Options Prices." *Journal of Business*, 51 (1978), 621-651.

Chaudhury, M. M., and J. Wei. "Upper Bounds for American Futures Options: A Note." *The Journal of Futures Markets*, 14 (1994), 111-116.

Cox, J. C., and S. A. Ross. "The Valuation of Options for Alternative Stochastic Processes." *Journal of Financial Economics*, 3 (1976), 145-166.

Longstaff, F. "Martingale Restriction Tests of Option Pricing Models." (version 1), Working paper, University of California, Los Angeles (1990).

Malz, A. M. "Using Option Prices to Estimate Realignment Probabilities in the European Monetary System." Federal Reserve Bank of New York Staff Reports, No.5, (September 1995).

Melick, W. R. and C. P. Thomas. "War and Peace: Recovering the Market's Probability Distribution of Crude Oil Futures Prices During the Gulf Crisis." Board of Governors of the Federal Reserve System International Finance Discussion Papers, No. 437 (October 1992).

Melick, W. R. and C. P. Thomas. "Using Options Prices to Infer PDFs for Asset Prices: An Application to Oil Prices During the Gulf Crisis." Board of Governors of the Federal Reserve System International Finance Discussion Papers, No. 541 (February 1996).

Neuhaus, H. "The Information Content of Derivatives for Monetary Policy: Implied Volatilities and Probabilities." Economic Research Group of the Deutsche Bundesbank Discussion Paper, No. 3/95 (July 1995).

Rubinstein, M. "Implied Binomial Trees." *Journal of Finance*, 49 (1994), 771-818.

Shimko, D. C. "Beyond Implied Volatility: Probability Distributions and Hedge Ratios Implied by Option Prices." Mimeo, Department of Finance and Business Economics, University of Southern California, (November 1991).

Chart 1
Canadian Financial Indicators

Exchange Rate

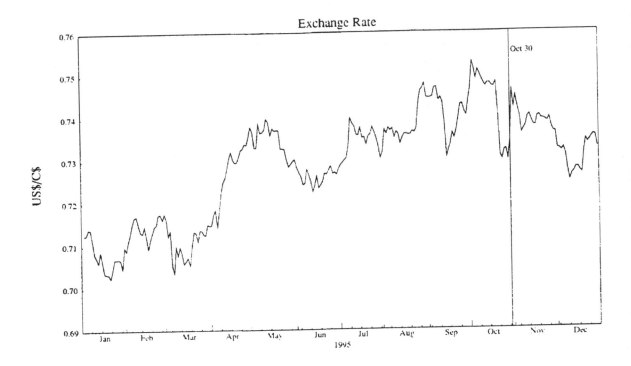

Interest rate differential

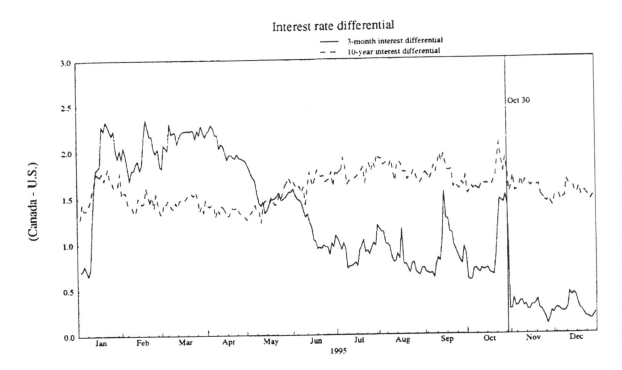

Chart 2
Canadian Financial Indicators

Exchange Rate

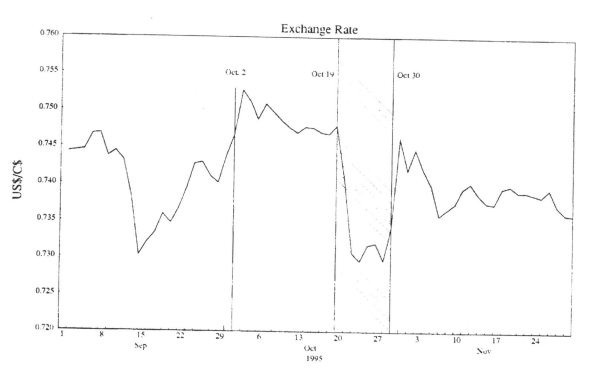

Interest rate differential

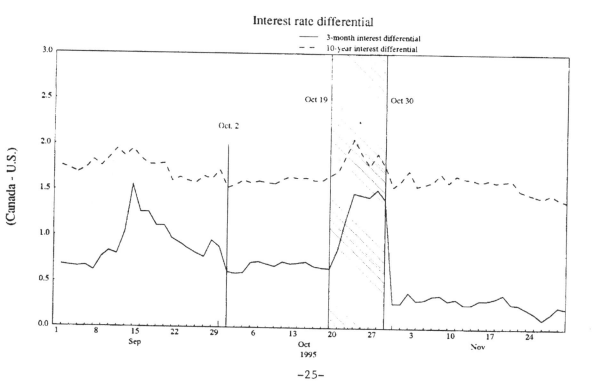

Chart 3
Implicit Distributions of the Canadian Dollar
Derived from December Options on the December 1995 contract

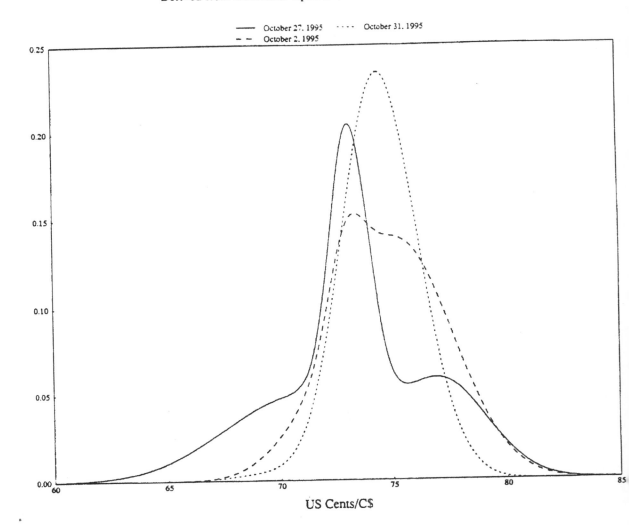

Date	Spot	Futures	Dispersion	Probability that futures rate on December 9, 1995 will be no more than:				
				67.50	70.00	72.50	75.00	78.50
10/2	74.76	74.74	6.60	.00	.03	.19	.55	.93
10/27	73.37	73.26	9.05	.06	.16	.36	.73	.93
10/31	74.53	74.44	4.26	.00	.01	.13	.62	.99

Note: Probabilities are risk-neutral or martingale-equivalent probabilities. Dispersion is the distance between 2/3 probability limits as a percent of the futures rate.

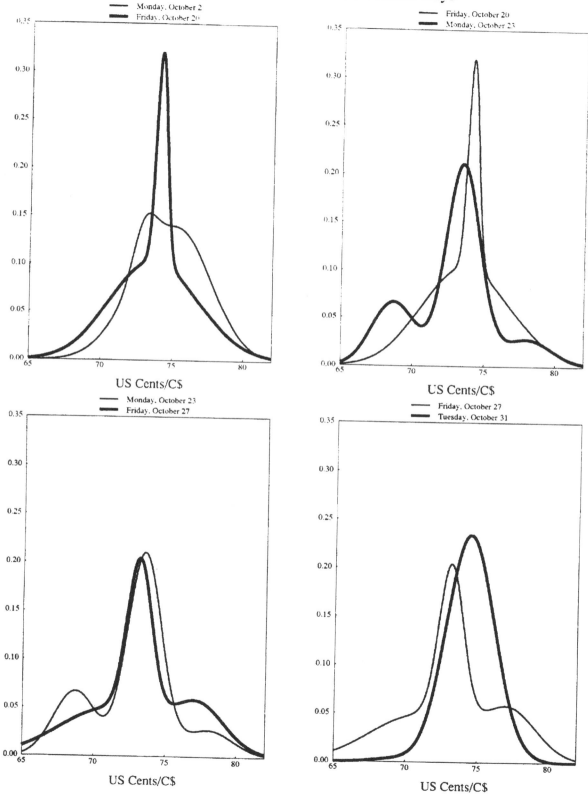

Chart 4
Comparison of Densities on Various Days

Chart 5
Comparison of Densities and Pricing Errors
October 2, 1995

Implicit Density Functions

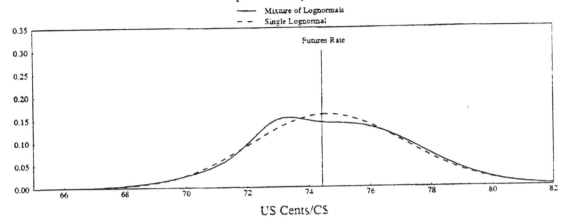

Call Pricing Errors

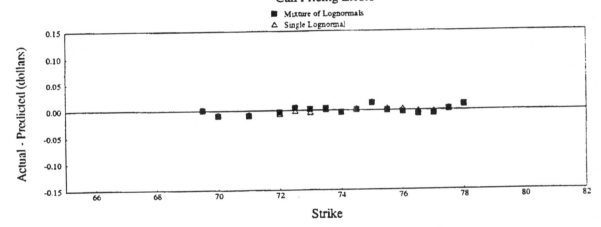

Put Pricing Errors

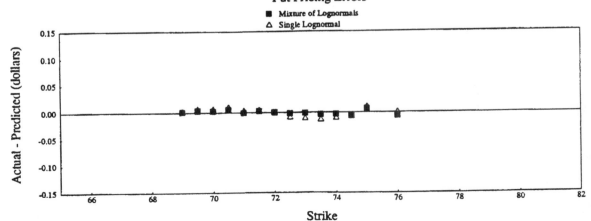

Chart 6
Comparison of Densities and Pricing Errors
October 20, 1995

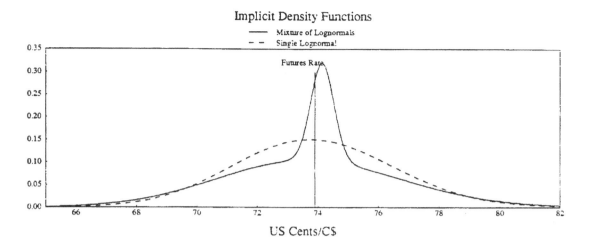

Implicit Density Functions

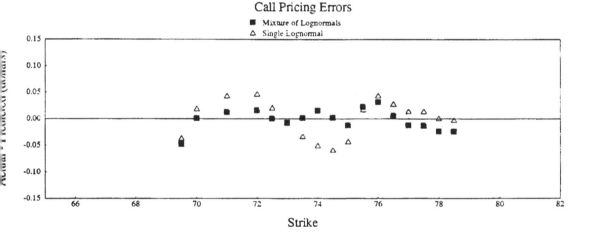

Call Pricing Errors

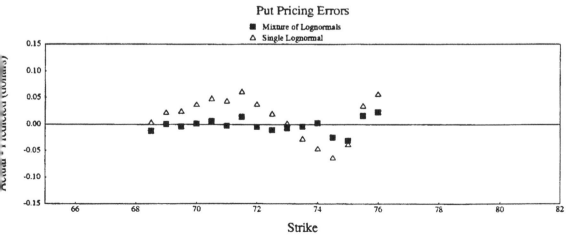

Put Pricing Errors

Chart 7
Comparison of Densities and Pricing Errors
October 23, 1995

Implicit Density Functions

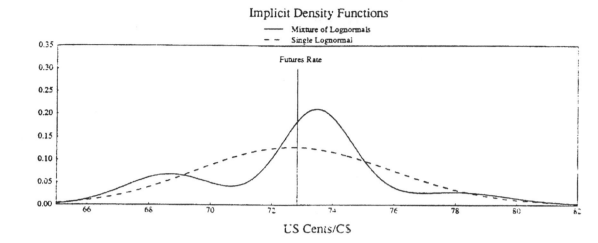

Call Pricing Errors

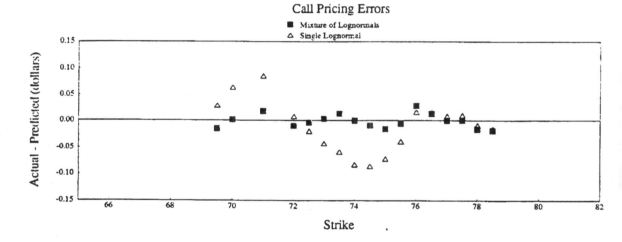

Put Pricing Errors

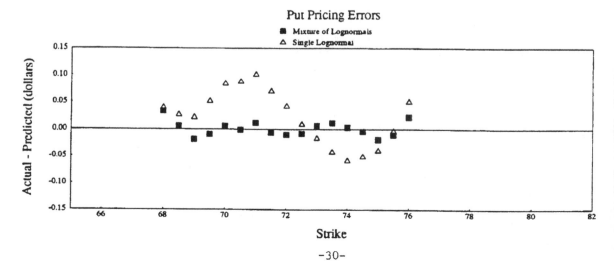

Chart 8
Comparison of Densities and Pricing Errors
October 27, 1995

Implicit Density Functions

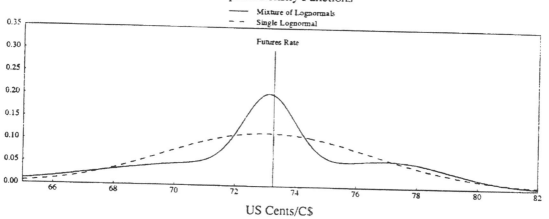

Call Pricing Errors

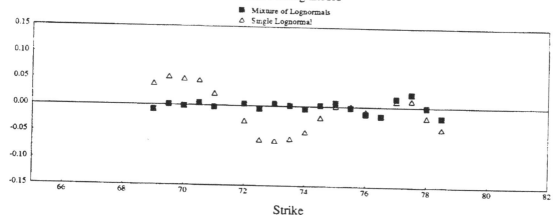

Put Pricing Errors

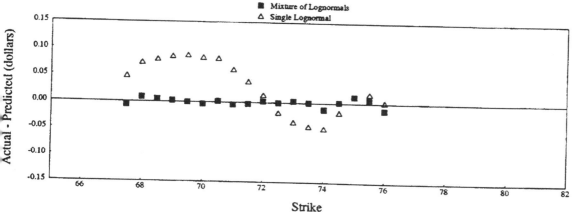

Chart 9
Comparison of Densities and Pricing Errors
October 31, 1995

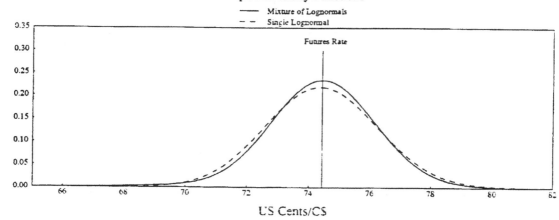

Implicit Density Functions

US Cents/C$

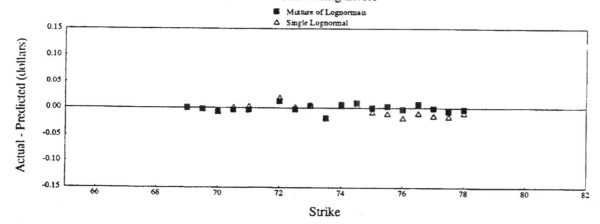

Call Pricing Errors

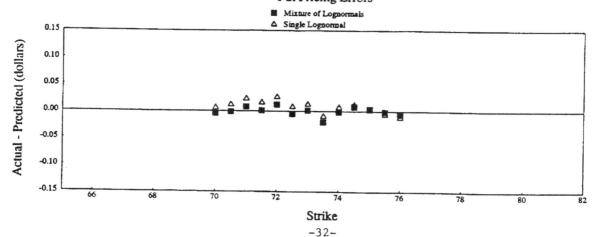

Put Pricing Errors

-32-

Lightning Source UK Ltd.
Milton Keynes UK
UKOW07f1855080915

258309UK00010B/379/P